If he can't stand someone,
he sends him to Leverkusen.
There at the end of the world.
He's put on ice forever.
(1896, grievance verse directed
at the boss, published in a tavern
newspaper on the occasion
of a scholars' drinking-fest at the
Elberfeld Dye Factory)

Until now the city has been known only more or less
regionally through such curiosities as the largest
stenographer club, or the highest (122 meters) administration
building in Germany—that of the Bayer Dye Factory.
(1969, the newspaper Die Welt)

Leverkusen is no longer a factory
that owns a city. (1969, Heinz Kühn,
Minister President of North-Rhine
Westphalia)

Strangers have always had difficulty with this city. Anyone
who wants to describe it, using the normal standards,
tends to find himself in a dilemma. Much here is so new,
so unusual, that ordinary words do not do it justice.
(1974, Professor Dr. Hannes Schmidt, Bonn-Bad Godesberg)

Quotes concerning the
growth and becoming of the city
of Leverkusen.

Dedicated to the memory of
Lord Mayor Wilhelm Dopatka, who
died 23 July 1979

compiled and written
by Werner A. Rudolph, photographed
by the Photo-Factory Leverkusen
as well as Karsten de Riese,
Thomas Höpker, Eric Schaal,
Brigitte Hellgoth, Gabriele Rudolph,
Jan-Bernd Donner, Christian
Dalchow, Bayer AG and others,
made into a book by
Rolf Müller Office,
produced by Brausdruck GmbH,
translated into English
by Harry B. Davis

and published by Verlag Brausdruck
Heidelberg
© Brausdruck GmbH, Heidelberg
first printing November 1981
ISBN 3-921524-32-6

**Pictures
and stories
from an unusual
city**

Leverkusen

4

Contrasts

"Rhine axis" is the name given to the row of bustling metropolises between Bonn and Duisburg, in whose center lies Leverkusen. Eyes are drawn to the industry and wharves along the river, which distract from the broad, green riverbanks. Nearby, the scene is dominated by modern residential areas and commercial districts. Old church spires and venerable facades seem to be suppressed and to lose their typicality. Even the natural setting of the Bergische Land, in whose spurs Leverkusen is embadded, seems at first glance to be nothing more than external frame. In fact it comprises many contrasts and includes a variegated mosaic.
The image of the city itself, however, is less stamped by any block pattern than by a blending of integral elements.
Long ago, many cities arose and grew here as people sought and found protection from external dangers. Leverkusen has one thing in common with them: a drawing-together due to external pressure–to fear of the large by the small. When in 1920 Wiesdorf, strengthened by industrial foundings, combined with Bürrig, there was already talk of an annexation urge on the part of Cologne. Nine years later, when Rheindorf, comprising 9,000 souls, merged with Wiesdorf, the appetite of the larger neighbor was already swollen. The city of Cologne spread out over the left riverbank, well beyond Rheindorf. In the east, in Schlebusch, the danger of being gobbled up was even greater. The community's own administration reached an agreement on incorporation with Cologne's city council. On May 12, 1929, 95 per cent of votes cast favored Wiesdorf. Not that the Schlebuschers or the Rheindorfers preferred to be Wiesdorfers rather the Cologners; they wanted to remain Schlebuschers and Rheindorfers.

5

6

Work and pleasures. Leverkusen has 89,000 jobs and 24 Carnival societies, no employment office of its own – but every year a Carnival prince is chosen and two Carnival parades are held. Regardless of the origins of its residents, the city cultivates customs of the Rhine area, while the residents of Leverkusen pursue countless hobbies in clubs and groups as well as privately. The jobs have lured people from all corners of the globe. They have brought with them not only their individuality but also their own interests.

8

Every day, rows of cars reminiscent of a state soccer match. During work hours some 14,000 cars are parked around the Bayer works. They and the considerable commercial vehicle traffic in the area led to the construction of efficient highways. But there are also kilometer-long paths for hiking ore carefree bicycling. Remote from heavy traffic, they tie the suburbs to each other and to the city center. Thus the "chemical city" has become a heaven for bicyclists—and that most assuredly includes work traffic.

Urban life and country idyll. The city tradition of Leverkusen is not old. When the birth of the 100,000th resident marked the transition to metropolis, Leverkusen hadn't even a city center. In the year following, the Council managed to make up for this oversight. Out of "the factory to which a town belongs" there emerged a city pulsing with life. The new business district is not only a shopping center; it is the focal point of cultural and social life–point of contact between the suburbs and their larger and smaller centers. Everything beyond this that has been decisive in shaping the character of this area–settled since the Stone Age–has, in many areas, and not only outlying ones, been maintained.

First impressions and contrasts

Water

Leverkusen is situated at the con-
fluence of the Rhine, Wupper
and Dhünn. The abundance of water
was utilized already in the 14th
Century to drive mills and forge
hammers. Five hundred years later it
became the basis on which the
chemical industry was built. It was
for this reason that Carl Leverkus
came here, in 1860, and Friedrich
Bayer, in 1891. Water is indis-
pensable for production, important
as a means of transportation. Today,
more water is used in Leverkusen
than in Hamburg, and – by weight –
about half the commercial transport
is carried out of the Rhine.

Land

Over its breadth of some 14 kilometers, the city rises from the low
terrace of the Rhine plain in the
west in three stages to the mountain-
ous suburbs in the east. Industry
is concentrated in the western
area of the city, in contrast to the
largely residential areas in the east
and northwest. Planning had to
proceed from the natural, charmingly
contradictory shapes of landscape,
which, till then, had been a corridor
of transit harboring little culture.

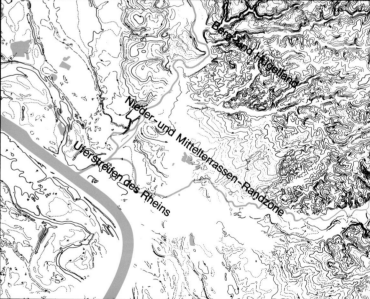

People

Leverkusen came into being through mergers. In 1920, Wiesdorf united with Bürrig and was accorded city rights. In 1930 were added Rheindorf, Schlebusch and Stein-büchel. The new name: Leverkusen. In 1955 the city became county-excepted, in 1963 attaining a population of 100,000. Thus it was a metropolis. In 1975, the new communal reapportioning led to the merging of Leverkusen with the cities of Opladen and Bergisch Neukirchen as well as the Monheim suburb Hitdorf. The artificially formed city area united cities and villages rich in tradition with new settlements built on the green like Alkenrath, Mathildenhof, Rheindorf-Nord and Steinbüchel-West. These are independent neighborhoods with their own infrastructure. The nearly 170,000 Leverkuseners do not constitute a homogeneous population. Only a few have resided here fore generations; most have arrived since the Second World War.

Factory

It started with Carl Leverkus. When the apothecary from Wermels-kirchen relocated his ultramarine factory on the Rhine, he confidently called his domain Leverkusen by Mülheim on the Rhine. But not until the settlement here of the factories of Friedrich Bayer & Co. for the production of anilin dyes did the ascent begin. Bayer acquired a large part of the Leverkusen works and transferred the main offices from Barmen to Wiesdorf. That was the origin of the international concern Bayer, which today employs 180,000 persons and does a business of nearly 26 billion German marks a year.

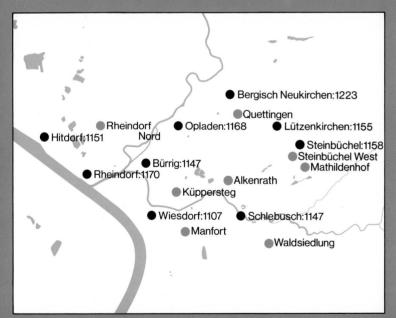

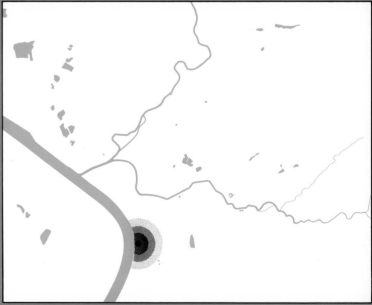

Roads

No metropolis in the Federal Republic of Germany is better served by autobahns and federal highways than Leverkusen. The autobahns Aachen–Wuppertal–Bremen (A 1) and Frankfurt–Oberhausen–Berlin (A 3) intersect in the heart of the city. Autobahn accesses over 2.5 square kilometers. A third autobahn coming from Düsseldorf intersects at Rheinallee. Together with the three federal highways that cross Leverkusen, this amounts to excellent trans-city connections. But it also entails many problems, for city planning as well as for environment. Much remains to be done, but the very pressure created by the problems has led to a number of model solutions.

Railway

Important and heavily traveled rail lines serve the metropolitan area. Cologne-Düsseldorf, via Wiesdorf, Küppersteg and Rheindorf; and Cologne-Wuppertal, via Schlebusch and Opladen. In addition there are local lines from Opladen to Düsseldorf and Remscheid-Lennep. Then there is a freight line connection, Cologne–Duisburg, with a freight station in Morsbroich. A central stop for passenger service, however, has existed only since 1979 – the station Leverkusen-Central, on the edge of the new business district. Directly adjacent is the bus terminal, from which all suburbs can be reached. Opladen (in the train schedule still without the addition of Leverkusen) is also of importance in long-distance travel, while the four additional stations serve their own areas and carry work traffic.

 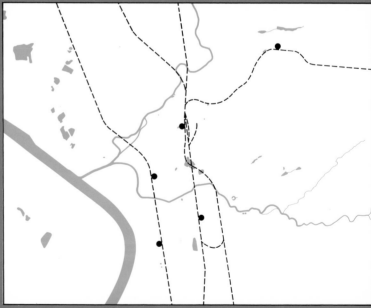

Dhünn

Tributary of the Wupper, says the lexicon. For Leverkusen it is more: a systematically broadening river meadow transversing the entire city area from east to west. Along this green backbone lie the city hospital, advanced schools, small and large sport facilities, the cultural center Forum, etc. The sport and leisure activity area can be easily and safely crossed by pedestrians and bicyclists without annoying intersections.

Center

The task was to provide a center for a number of scattered individual communities. "It must be the focal point not only for the administration but also for commercial, intellectual and cultural life. It must not arise 'on the fringes' but rather must lie at the crossroads of the city. Always within consciousness, at the same time undisturbed by vehicle traffic, a zone for pedestrians. Near the hub of Leverkusen, the Bayer works, but not overshadowed by it." This is how the city center was described in the official opinion drawn up in 1958/59 by Professors Guther and Hillebrecht. On this basic the city center was built on the "densest" point of the city, neither in the geographic center, nor in the center of population gravity but extremely accessible.

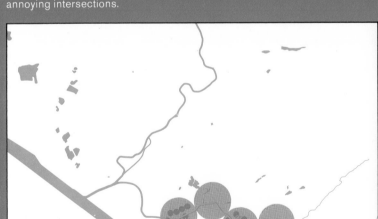

Stock-taking

City with Pasts

A young industrial city cannot boast centuries of history. But the area it encompasses – the communities that make up the city – they have a past. Leverkusen has pasts.

Whoever looks into the few existing history books solely by local authors will find no dates of historical battles or epoch-making foundings. Instead he will read of fiefs with which the Counts of Berg rewarded their knights, and properties of the Abbeys of Altenberg and Deutz. The region between Cologne and the former residence cities of Düsseldorf and Burg on the Wupper partook of – and endured, often enough – the history of others.
And so little of great historical significance issued from the noble old edifices which have lived on into our time.

Morsbroich Castle became known outside the local region only in the middle of this century, when it came to house the city museum with its exhibits of contemporary at. Originally it was a fief received in the 13th century by a knight with the epithet "Moor". The Herrenhaus (manor), newly constructed in 1774 in late rococo style, belonged for nearly two hundred years to the Teutonic Knights and for a hundred years to the family of the Baron of Diergardt. The city of Leverkusen acquired it from him.
Situated above the Wupper Plain, the Friedenberger Hof, with its distinctive staircase tower, was frequently the residence of important dignitaries. Of regional importance is the little Rittersitz, or Knight's Residence (which finally was a small peasant's castle), because a connection was established between it and Evirhardus of Upladhin, who was mentioned in a document dated 1168. It was from the name Upladhin – which means "on the mountain slope" – that the place-name Opladen developed. The Friedenberger Hof, which was completely renovated from 1965 to 1971, today houses an art collection. The former residence of Jacob of Omphal recalls the architecture of the 16th century. Omphal, doctor of both German and Roman law, occasionally lived in Haus Büchel, which accounts for its popular name

"Doktorsburg". A humanist and statesman, he had properties scattered throughout the Rhineland; but he was buried in the Wiesdorf Church, by his own request, 1567. Today the Doktorsburg, situated on the edge of the city park, is the most prominent of the older houses.
More antiquities of this sort could be listed, giving the lie to the rumor of Leverkusen as a place without history – such as Aldegundis Church, in Rheindorf, which in former times was apparently united with the Castle. The parish is often mentioned in old documents. Anyone searching for traces of ancient city history will in addition come upon a period of some 450 years during which most of the area encompassed by the present-day city was a single entity.
Parish Miselohe of that time was not an entity that was or should have been able to act on its own initiative. Count Gerhard of Berg formed the parishes about 1360 more for the purpose of gathering taxes and revenue.
The first assay toward self-administration was the work of none other than Napoleon, when, at the beginning of the 19th century, he established the French administrative system here. Among others, Opladen and Schlebusch were singled out as administrative centers. The Congress of Vienna made mayoralities of these municipalities, as the French had

Opladen: Etching from 1840.

called them. In addition, Opladen, Schlebusch, Monheim and Richrath came to constitute (1816) the county of Opladen, which three years later was combined with the county of Solingen.

In 1896–that is, 77 years later–Solingen was exempted from the county, and the county seat was moved to Opladen.

But it was not until 1914 that the administrative apparatus was transferred to the newly constructed building on the Frankenberg. Opladen remained the "capital of the county" when, in the course of territorial restructuring in 1929/30, Wupper County and the City of Leverkusen were simultaneously created. The city name as such first appeared with the fusion of Wiesdorf, Rheindorf, Schlebusch and Steinbüchel. But does this constitute the actual birth of Leverkusen?

It is a moot point when the history of the city began. Was it in 1862 when the apothecary Dr. Carl Leverkus moved to the Rhine with his Wermelskirchen establishment and named the site "Leverkusen" in honor of his ancestors, after his family residence near (Remscheid-) Lennep? Or did it not begin until 1891 when Bayer from Elberfeld came to Wiesdorf? From then on, hundreds of families poured into the village. With them they brought a full measure of problems with which the responsible members of the neighboring communities–themselves a part of the industrial migration– had to deal. Self-confidence increased as economic power grew. In 1920 Wiesdorf and Bürrig merged, thereby blocking the beginning of a "willingness to help" signaled from Cologne. Ten years later, the fledgling Wiesdorf, together with Schlebusch, Steinbüchel and Rheindorf, once again eluded the threatening embrace. They combined to form a new city, and the aggregate was now called Leverkusen. That was on 1 April 1930. The step to metropolis was not made until after World War II, however. The number of jobs, and inhabitants, soared. Ten years after the war, in 1955, Leverkusen was county-exempted.

A mere two years later, independence was again in danger. But it now became apparent that the populace–brought together from all corners of the earth–was already unified. The ardor with which they backed the citizen-initiative "LEV must live" came as a surprise to many. On the other hand, the county-city Opladen quite naturally wanted to survive too. The population there had grown enormously also, the newly-arrived now firmly a part of the traditional city-consciousness. The state legislature of North-Rhine-Westphalia made its decision in September 1974: "The cities of Leverkusen, Opladen and Bergisch Neukirchen"–so read the text of the law–"will be combined in one new county-exempted city. The city will be called Leverkusen." And further, "Hitdorf, from the community of Monheim, will be incorporated into the city of Leverkusen." The second birth of the city was thus not entirely voluntary. Nevertheless, the Council and city administration of Opladen soon thereafter spoke out for looking ahead rather than backward and for a readiness to tackle new tasks. The course of the new Leverkusen was thus staked out...

17

The Rhine floods its banks: 1920.   Bayer: Gate 1: 1912.

The Many Pasts.

Leverkusen: building and more building

When the time of the Iron Crosses ended, 1945, the people of Leverkusen erected a wrought-iron cross nearly ten meters high in front of their Municipal Building. A memorial to the war dead. The iron came from dud bombs. The city had little other possibility to put the past to work. It had to look forward. Along with the 12,000 citizens who returned from the evacuation there came 6,500 refugees from the eastern territories in those early, difficult years. By 1946 the population had passed the pre-war figure of 49,000 to hit 55,000, and by 1950 the figure was 65,000, The situation was similar in the neighboring cities of Opladen, Bergisch Neukirchen and Hitdorf (which now belong to Leverkusen), if not quite so grave.

About 1,100 of the 14,000 dwellings had been destroyed in the war, and three out of four houses damaged. Reconstruction thus became the first task; but it had little effect on the housing shortage. The influx of people continued, some 3,000 each year. In 1960 the figure was 5,000. Thousands, of new dwellings merely sufficed to keep the huge demand at a bearable level. The city puffed itself up, reached into land reserves and built settlements the size of small cities. Great building sites became typical for Leverkusen. Between 1954 and 1958, Alkenrath emerged, on fields and meadows, along forest edges – 2,600 dwellings, schools, churches, kindergartens, market squares and streets. It was the prototype of a neighborhood of the kind planners envisioned for communities of between 5,000 and 8,000 inhabitants. Mathildenhof followed, in a lovely landscape of rolling hills, while in Rheindorf building was going on at 48 sites simultaneously. The huge project Rheindorf-Nord, with 4,000 dwellings, was begun in 1960 – three years later, on the other end of the city, the settlement Steinbüchel-West. The extent of building activity was marveled at by outsiders, the implied financial strength regarded with suspicion. Dedications of new construction became commonplace. Neighboring observers gasped. But they failed to recognize that an enormous need was being met. Hospitals arose where only schools had housed sick-beds. But there was also a shortage of schools. And so higher-level schools grew up along with grade schools being built in the suburbs. When the city finally became free to create the useful, in addition to essential, it finally was catching up with smaller and "poorer" cities. Thus Leverkusen already had a population of 95,000 when the first indoor swimming pool was opened. Features already possessed by other towns, such as a centrally located municipal building, cultural and shopping facilities, were still missing.

Before these could be begun, other, more pressing, facilities had to be built. Building sites became commonplace in Leverkusen – sites for roads, bridges and buildings. Until finally the area in which the city center would arise swarmed with cranes and bulldozers. In 1962, five years before construction began, Wilhelm Westecker, in his book "The Rebirth of the German Cities," published by Econ-Verlag, marveled:

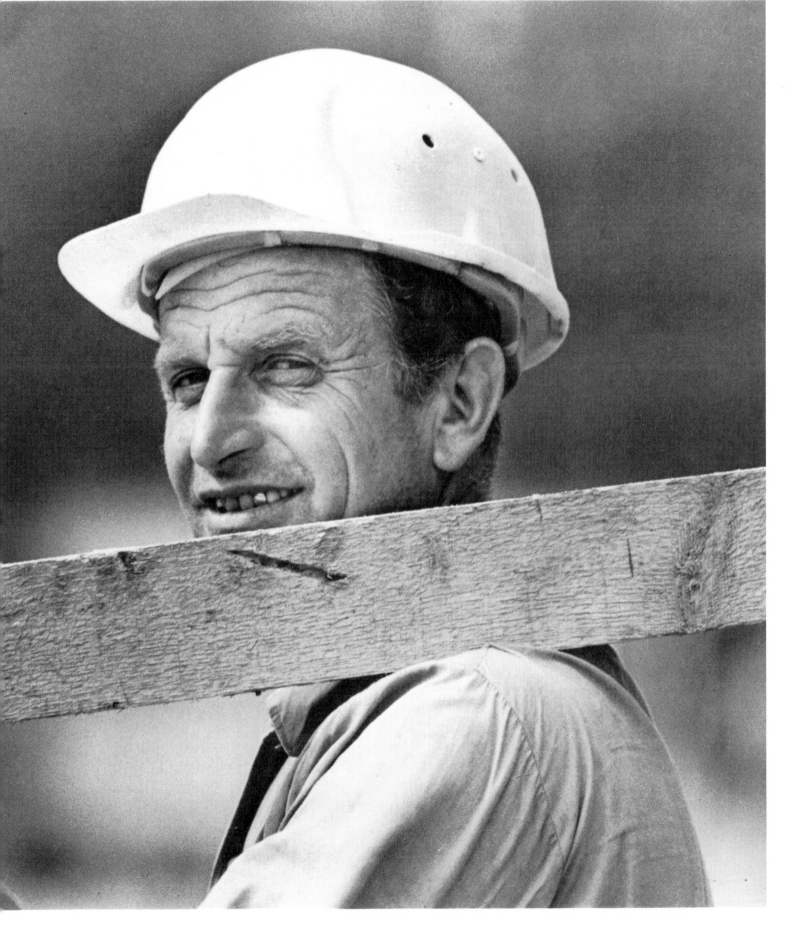

The future, as seen by construction people in the first decade of this century, lasted exactly 61 years. The town hall, first occupied in 1910, had a short but checkered history. For ten years it was the seat of the mayoralty of Küppersteg, then administrative center for the community of Wiesdorf–merged with Bürrig–which became a city in 1921. In 1930 it became the town hall of the newly founded city of Leverkusen. On 25 October 1971 the building was razed.

Bridging the Rhine. It measured more than a kilometer long, the construction site where the auto-bahn bridge arose that was required by A1 running from Bremen via Münster and Wuppertal to Aachen. When the bridge was opened to traffic 5 July 1965, Levekusen became one of the most important transport junctions in Germany.

On 1 April 1977 the new town hall for Leverkusen was completed, following three years of construction. Together with its imaginatively conceived plaza and underground garage, it constituted the corner-stone and axis of the business district.

Aerial photos:
Courtesy of the Regierungspräsidium of Düsseldorf
No. 19/30/2662 and No. 19/14/827

20

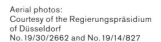

"The miracle seems to be coming true that one of the newest German cities will soon have a contiguous, modern city center of a scope not achieved by many city, not even the cities that were destroyed, nor the metropolises with architecturally historic old-quarters." But he also saw "How much this industrial city, with its scattered residential areas, needs a city center." And so it was neither the mere desire to build nor delight in the new that produced Leverkusen's immense building activity. No matter when any particular construction started, it should actually have been completed by that time. The same principle prevails today, though there is nothing that can be called population growth. Projects that had to be left undone during the hectic development of the first three post-war years are now overdue. Considering the huge building achievement and the press of time involved, the few evident weakpoints are of little consequence. Everything has been done to meet the needs of human beings. And since these are subject to change, the adage applies that "Anyone who builds a road has many masters."

21

Leverkusen: Building and More Building.

The grace of modern technology in the dusk:
autobahn bridge near Leverkusen.

22

For more than 400 years the Hitdorf ferry connected the two banks of the Rhine. Of the three ferries that formerly plied the Rhine here, this is the only one still in operation.

Everyone who thinks of cities like Cologne, Koblenz, Neuss, Bonn or Düsseldorf immediately connects them with the Rhine. Why not also Leverkusen? This city, which many vaguely imagine to lie in the Ruhr, is totally dependent on its location on a river. The chemical industry sought an abundance of water for its technical needs as well as its need for commercial transport. But that happened only in the middle of the 19th century, when other Rhine cities could look back on a rich tradition. But there is historical significance here too, even if one mistrusts the most recent historical research. According to it, it was not at Worms but at the Leverkusen suburb of Hitdorf that the Nibelungs crossed the Rhine. And it is only legend that has the present-day suburb of Rheindorf as the point from which the Frankish king Pippin the Short departed on his many journeys. But there is a foundation to the centuries-old tradition of the ferries. The Wiesdorf ferry existed at the time of the Romans, and at times during the Middle Ages it was the most important ferry between Cologne and Düsseldorf. Not

until the construction of the autobahn bridge did its clientele so diminish that, in 1969, it ceased operation. Erwin Menz doubtless foresaw the future when, in his book "Young City on the Great Stream", published in 1961, he wrote: "A trip over the concrete ribbon of the future autobahn bridge can never fully replace a boat ride across the stream." Still, this experience with another ferry, that at Rheindorf, had already ceased to be possible. It had closed down in 1954, after a few years of operation "according to need". All that is left is the car-ferry between Leverkusen-Hitdorf and Cologne-Langel, although it too no longer pays its own way. But the tradition lives on, a tradition stretching back 400 years. This ferry offered the shortest distance between the roads Elberfeld–Hitdorf and Cologne–Neuss. For that reason it had outdistanced its competition as early as 1830. The three ferry stations additionally served, until the outbreak of World War I, as mooring points fot the "Müllemer Böötche" (steamships from Mülheim on the Rhine – today Cologne–Mülheim). In the meantime, a small dock has been built

24

in Leverkusen-Wiesdorf; but the relationship of Leverkuseners to the Rhine sooner finds expression in the three
yacht harbors – one in Wiesdorf and two larger ones in
Hitdorf – which have a picturesque backdrop of centuries-old
house facades. Only 1,600 meters of the 8,200 meters of
harbor front in Leverkusen have an industrial backdrop.
One section is dominated by roads. But the largest part of the
river bank is green. It largely retains its natural character
but is to be opened for foot and bicycle paths. Leverkusen
not only profits from the Rhine, it lives on it as well.

...and it's on the Rhine afterall.

City tour along the water

The gentleman on the bicycle doesn't make a sporty impression, even though he's obviously put a good deal of money into his casual appearance. It must have seemed bored to him, or at least ready to chat. In any case he pushed his brand-new bike toward me, stood it awkwardly on the Wupper bank and superfluously remarked that cycling was his hobby. He said he'd found the path along the Rhine somewhat bumpy but charming nevertheless. I confirmed its charm.

Now he wanted to go to Altenberg, he said in an adventurous tone. "There's supposed to be a bike path straight through Leverkusen", he added with a somewhat doubtful note.

I could only partially confirm this. "Not all the way to Altenberg", I said, "but a good piece nevertheless". "We'll see", said the gentleman. And I had a picture of him – mid-forties, faultless sport clothes, sitting very straight peddling along the fresh, undulating Wupper meadow. I saw him already on the Dhünn dike on the edge of the artificially laid-out water landscape, and imagined I could feel his irritation at the high towers of the purification plant to his right and the concrete ribbon of the autobahn ahead. "Looks like there will be hills", the man says, and I feel I must pacify him. "No, it's all very flat, and you won't be bothered by cars either."

"No, over there", he responds. And he points to the green slopes opposite, some 10 to 20 meters high. "On, those – no", I correct him, "those aren't hills; they're just the planted areas around a depot".

"A trash-dump", he says.

"I guess you could call it that, but it's well disguised, even if it should grow bigger."

"Is there nothing here that's genuine then, nothing that's grown naturally?" said the gentleman angrily, toying with his gear-shift.

"Little", I confessed, "neither the people nor much of nature have grown up here over generations. The mouth of the Wupper was laid out artificially- originally it was somewhere else. But Rheindorf there ahead is genuine; it's still pretty much as it was centuries ago, at least the old village. On the other hand, most Rheindorfers live in new settlements."

The gentleman with the creases in his knickers seemed to be slightly confused, and asked, "Is that the way there?" and hurried away with short steps, although the Wupper meadow is perfectly flat.

I wasn't exactly unhappy to be rid of the worry-wart. I waited for a while, then peddled off in the same direction on my collapsible bike.

I overtook him. "Oh, it's you", he said. "You could have told me you were going to follow me". Except for an embarrassed "Could I have?" nothing reasonable occurred to me.

"Do you want to ride farther with me?" I'd expected and feared this question, but I had no excuse ready at hand.

"Is that the new city?" he asked a little later, pronouncing it

"Sitti" with a sonorous z like most Leverkuseners, and
at that point I should have noticed something. I answered that
from here, from the bank of the little river Dhünn, only a
suggestion of the city could be had, even though it was
quite close. "A lot of concrete," he countered, and it sounded
like a challenge.
I became testy. "Well, the old formula of stone upon stone
doesn't exactly apply anymore. A few years ago that style was
called objective or honest or something like that."
"Was that a style?"
Now I was really becoming angry. "You're pretty quick with
your judgement. Don't you think a person should take a closer
look at things before he judges? When you get closer you'll
see that it's more inviting – and practical – and there's little
disturbance from cars." For a moment I hoped the aggressive
tone would frighten him off. That wouldn't displease me at
all. But he only asked, "Are you coming along with me?" –
didn't wait for my answer but was already back on his saddle.
I don't know why I rode along with him or why I called out:
"Behind the railway underpass to the right, and then left."
Of course, I'd succeeded in dodging his question. But the
next one came soon enough. "Are the Olympic sportsmen
trained here?" – full of irony as we went by the first sports
field.
"Yes, some."
"What? And the others are bought ready-made?" His laugh
was too thick for my taste. "No, others are in another club,
and it trains on another field!" I didn't bother to go into the
fine differences between the two clubs, which held a string
of championships and records, both with a 04 after their
club name and both subsidized by Bayer AG. Every question
avoided seemed a gain. "Are all the sports facilities connected with Bayer?" – still another question.
"No." I took a deep breath. "A few sports areas and the indoor
and outdoor pools belong to the city", I said, making on the
man no noticeable impression. "The bicycle paths, the
bridges and the regulation of the Dhünn also have nothing
to do with Bayer." And I went on, just to be safe: "Besides
that, if you look over to the right you'll see the Wuppermann
Works, another Leverkusen firm with a rich tradition."

"I suspected as much. The stream looked much better when
it was unregulated!" The guy was incorrigible. And so I
decided to ride on in silence, enjoying the family gardens
in bloom, the huge field of grain to the left of the path, at
which we overtook a strolling family with baby-buggy. At this
point I noticed that my companion was silent.
"Behind the railway bridge to the right we'll go through the
Morsbroicher Forest to the Castle" – I murmered this in
passing. "What is it good for?" and it again sounded too
penetrating.
"One part of the Castle is several hundred years old, after
all, and besides that it has been our Museum for Modern Art
for decades. The city intends to renovate and expand it."
"Do you understand modern art?" harped the man. I said one
had to try to understand it, that one couldn't always expect

28

something beautiful, something decorative – it was a lot like city construction. Everyone expected something beautiful, usually something green, and nevertheless streets that are never jammed – but theaters all the same, department stores and so on. What then really comes is something that everyone pretends not to have wanted, something that should have been much better. "But ride on in!" I wound up. I'd said enough anyway.

"No", said my tedious friend, suddenly quite friendly, "I'm going left, to Alkenrath. I've lived there many years and I'm quite content. I just wanted to try out my new bike today, and I wanted to find out what other people think about Leverkusen, the green areas and the new features. Who really knows his own city after all? So long, and don't be too angry with me."

In a young city the few scattered, remaining antiquities occupy a special status. A number of giant trees have been designated natural monuments.

City tour along the water.

Mosaic of Facades

For a time, they were passed off as having no style, the houses with the peaked gables, the imitation half-timber and the casual window patterns. At that time the facades were covered with monotonous stucco. Now, shapes and forms have been brought out by carefully chosen colors.

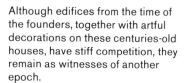

Although edifices from the time of the founders, together with artful decorations on these centuries-old houses, have stiff competition, they remain as witnesses of another epoch.

The span of architecture in Leverkusen extends from medieval house and castle construction, as it is to be seen in Morsbroich, to the functional orientation of modern concrete. Scarcely was the fascination of the possibilities in successive building styles realized, than sobriety became more sober and encouraged the quest for more playful facades.
And not only in Leverkusen.

32

Fantasy in wood and half-timber, on the one hand, and in concrete and synthetic materials on the other. Taste and skill obviously have little to do with either money or size, with materials or with technical progress. One simply has to have them, not only to achieve constructional ends but also to please the eye and to create atmosphere.

The great hall of the cultural center, the Forum.

August-Wilhelm-Hofmann Street

A morning, midday and evening on a day and in a street like many others.
Not far from the business district and the huge firm that made it possible, the idyl remains;
the human being, with his everyday customs and wants, seems to be the measure of all things.
Developments all around seem to have been excluded.

34

6 o'clock.

8 o'clock.

35

3 p.m.

6 p.m.

36

8 p.m.

10 p.m.

37

They continue to be typical for Leverkusen, the Bayer-owned settlements with free-standing, two-story buildings, surrounded by small gardens. They are still called "colonies," and are distinguished from each other only by Roman numerals. Traffic noise causes only a little disturbance in these oases with their stands of old trees, curving streets, small squares and freshly painted facades and half-timber gables. Situated in the central area of a metropolis, the colonies undoubtedly constitute an unusual monument to the recent past.

August-Wilhelm-Hofmann Street.

From Aunt Emma to the City

There were Aunt Emmas everywhere. The small towns and villages from which Leverkusen emerged also had a "colonial wares" store just around the corner. There were the main-streets where the baker and butcher, the smith and locksmith, the carpenter and electrician offered their assistance – today called services. They grew and changed and became shopping centers such as are found in a place like Schle-busch, or, more so, in Opladen. In former county seats, the department store and the branch store augmented shopping possibilities – pedestrian zones facilitated window-shopping (small photo on opposite page).

This kind of organic growth is impossible in entirely new residential areas. But in Leverkusen the city planned the city centers along with the dwellings. There you find not only shopping areas; you find also churches and their satellited facilities, schools and kindergartens, market square, bank, library, and about every fixture that belongs to everyday life – all grouped together.

And yet – when someone in Leverkusen said, "I'm driving into town", it wasn't long ago that he meant the neighbor city of Cologne, or Düsseldorf. As late as 1969, 70 pfennigs of every mark of buying power drained into these metropolises. That was one of the reasons why Leverkusen decided to build a City Center, a feat which in terms of financial outlay, political engagement and architectural conception is un-equaled in the Federal Republic of Germany. A continuous pedestrian zone about 600 meters wide and 600 long is an open invitation to carefree strolling, shopping, lingering. The distance to underground parking areas, to buses and trains, is short.

39

40

Nine weekly markets give a lively
aspect to old and new city districts.
To a considerable extent, the wares
stem from Leverkusens farmers,
who also offer their produce for sale
right at their farmsteads.
The "industrial city" is, to a large
extent, self-sufficient.

They have taken over some of the functions of Aunt Emma's store, these kiosks or "Büdchen" as the local people call them.

For it's not as it used to be that people stop here merely for a bottle of "pop" or a bag of sweets. Whether walking to school, to work, or simply taking a stroll – without the colorful "Büdchen" things wouldn't be half as pleasant.

From the City to Aunt Emma.

The Many Professions
Between the exacting precision
work on massive steel parts and
a hobby like hand-weaving,
there is a world of difference–or
perhaps only a couple of intervening
streets. The modern city is a micro-
cosmos of our society with its many
occupations. It's the same for
Leverkusen, although almost half of
the positions here are connected
with the chemical industry.
But even here there is variety.

42

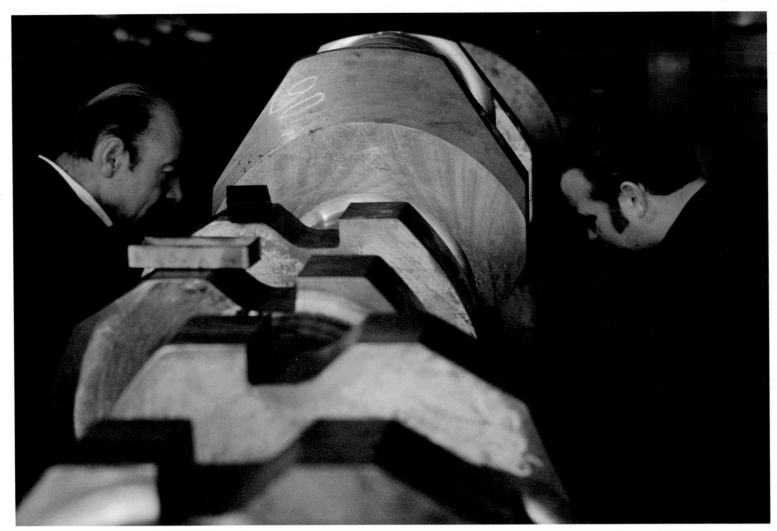

An indication of how different the
occupations are is the fact that, at
Bayer alone, there is a choice of
50 professional specialties.
A further indicator is the fact that
every 20th employee of the firm has
completed work at a university,
and every 12th works in research.
In Leverkusen, where, in addition to
a number of scientific research
laboratories, extensive technical
labs and experimental facilities are
located, the figures are even higher.
Beyond this, photo-chemistry is

represented by Agfa-Gevaert, with its many specialties. This European firm, formed in 1964 by the fusion of Gevaert Photo-Products N.V. (Mortsel/Belgium) and Agfa AG (Leverkusen), has its administration and a main works here. Additionally, the city is the home of significant intermediate industry. A good example is Wuppermann GmbH, from which the adjacent photo (left) stems; others are Textar GmbH for brake and clutch linings, Kronos-Titan, Eumuco Machine Construction, Denso Chemicals, Schusterinsel Textile Finishing, Imbau, Illbruck Foam Materials Technology and Goetze Rubber Works. Finally, the Federal Railway Maintenance Plant is among the largest employers. In contrast, the number of those engaged in the services is one third, noticeably lower than the federal average. But precisely here the trend is upward, a fact traceable not least of all to the development of retail trade.

On the whole the quality of jobs available is very high, and the good chances of advancement are guaranteed by the large size of the firms. It is for that reason that wages and salaries average a third higher than in the rest of the Federal Republic. Who can then wonder that there is little fluctuation in the level of employment?

43

The largest service organization in
Leverkusen is the city administration
itself. In many areas there is no real
"administering". It is more accurate
to speak of more than four thousand
fellow-workers active in more than
120 professions.

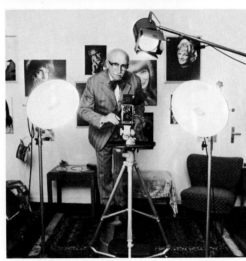

45

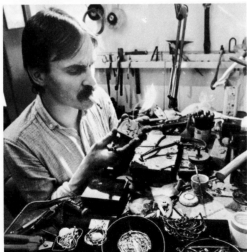

Few people have any idea of the many jobs and possibilities for earning a living in a city like Leverkusen.

The many professions.

Bayer and Leverkusen

When it comes to Bayer, the situation in the Leverkusen city council changes. Then, it is said, those members who are employed by the chemical concern are no longer objective. And so, a city ordinance provides for their exclusion in deliberations related to Bayer. There was a time that the majority frequented the city parliament when interests of the huge industrial works were at stake. In a city in which almost half of all jobs are in the chemical industry, and most of these in one firm, things are a bit different. Is it indeed possible to have independent city policies under such conditions?

The question is as old as the industrial settlement of the Rhine, older, that is, than Leverkusen itself. When the "Elberfelder Farben Factories, formerly Friedr. Bayer & Co", gradually transferred its operations from the Bergische Land to Kahlberg, the community of Wiesdorf, whose center was farther south, had a population of 2,512. Suddenly the figure rose steeply, and the many people who poured into the village didn't find what they were accustomed to and what they needed. There were no dwellings or shops, no theater or other facilities for communal life. Jokes circulated which had their boss, the chemist, sending people he didn't like to Leverkusen. But he, Dr. Carl Duisberg, for his part, saw to it that the industrial area was so outfitted with roads and railways that rapidly rising needs were met for decades to come. He had to do a good deal beyond this to insure that the workers lured here would stay on. He had dwellings built that were far superior to the tenements that had been built elsewhere, had a movie theater and recreation center built which still today find good use. Duisberg, who later would become an honorary citizen of Leverkusen, had complete freedom in these matters, not only because the burgomaster's office scarcely offered an alternative but also because of the three-class voting system. That disturbed many influential citizens. After World War I, Wiesdorf and Bürring were merged, and peaceful years of construction followed, particularly in the dwelling and school sectors. Expanding industry, however, raised issues that required new mergers. The firm was active in areas above and beyond its own production concerns; conflicts were unavoidable. Then came the world economic crisis, and everyone became concerned with his own narrower interests. The Nazi period and the war not only brought physical destruction; the IG Farben Concern was broken up. For a long time, Bayer and the city were doubtful of the future. Each saw itself as destined to be bound up with the other, until the new beginning brought about a disengagement as well a development no one had expected.

The following hectic period of buildup brought frictions between the city, which took communal self-government seriously, and its largest and most prestigious taxpayer. In retrospect, the effect was like the clearing of the air after a storm, and what ensued was a real partnership. The firm had long since realized that a functioning communal entity was essential to its own interests. And the City Council and city administration both realize their debt to those who work in this industrial complex. Out of the enterprise that began on the kitchen stove of the dye tradesman Friedrich Bayer there grew up a corporation of 63,000 employees. World-wide the firm employs more people than the total population of Leverkusen. On the 3.4-square-kilometer area occupied by the parent concern, with more than 600 buildings, there operates one of the largest and many-faceted production facilities for chemicals in Europe. Leverkusen is by no means Bayer, but Leverkusen without Bayer would be unthinkable.

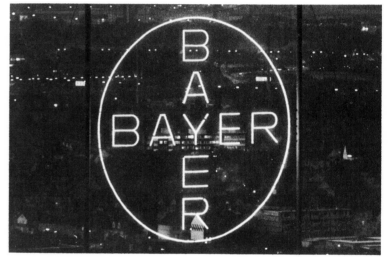

Of the 280,000 brand symbols registered with the German Patent Office, the Bayer cross is among the oldest and best known. Registered in 1904, the symbol was designed by Hans Schneider, an employee from Elberfeld. At first no one knew quite what to make of it, because there was hesitancy to abandon the roaring Bayer lion. After it was stamped on tablets in 1910, however, the development toward the best known international brand mark began.

46

Play of lines and forms: in the statue "Zyklopenthan" in front of the Bayer high-rise, but also dictated by technology in the production plant.

More than half of those who work "at Bayer" say it as if the founder were still alive—working in the Leverkusen firm. At the main branch of the firm the number of white-collar workers is higher than that of blue-collar workers.

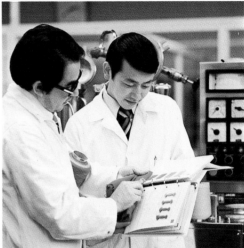

49

Bayer and Leverkusen.

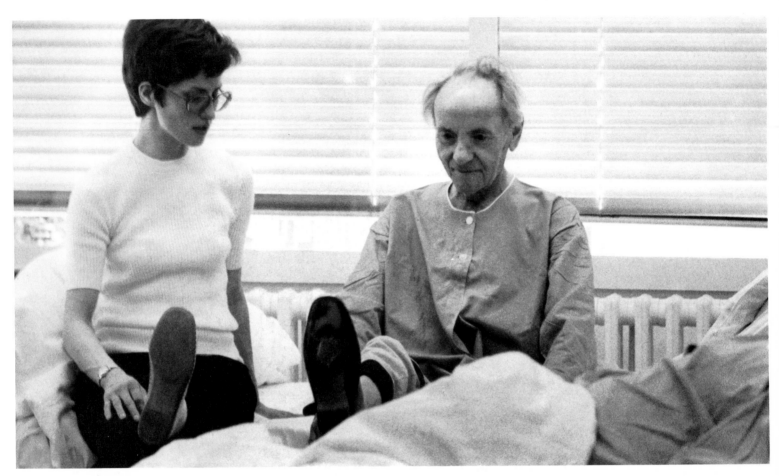

50

The 108 beds in the geriatric clinic of the City Hospital do not constitute a home for the aged. All efforts here are bent toward enabling the patients to return to normal life.

It pays to be skeptical about "the good old times", but one thing about them is probably certain: For his entire life, the individual lived within the security of the family circle. But industrial society creates generation gaps. Anyone who has never worked, or no longer does, is put on his own – more than ever before. The problem of youth is particularly serious in a young city. Construction and expansion of kindergartens and schools has been a continuing task over two decades. Owing to unceasing change, it is almost never completed, even though Leverkusen is frequently held up as a shining example in this regard. Five of the six high schools, as well as the consolidated school, were built new. The picture is about the same for other types of schools. At the same time, 45 youth centers were built, primarily by the parishes but also by private enterprise and the city. Then there were other facilities for youth, an interesting example of which is the adventure playground. Wish and will meanwhile continue.

51

Creative development through play
is the goal of pedagogically
attended playgrounds.

On the other hand, many Leverkuseners were thrown into their new home at an advanced age, into a new life devoid of familiar surroundings and old friends. And so, paradoxically, assistance for the aged was given special emphasis in this young city; new facilities were tested here. Among them was a trial geriatric clinic specially equipped to treat very old patients. In addition to the long-term treatment of acute illnesses, the goal is to maintain or restore physical mobility. The patient is to return to his accustomed way of life; and it is precisely toward this end that all assistance for the aged is concentrated: as much and as long as possible, an individual way of life is maintained. Thus the special programs such as theater subscriptions for the aged, recuperation activities and meals-on-wheels. Courses and lectures at a central facility in the Doktorsburg find a lively resonance. A special magazine, "The Eyeglasses", goes quarterly to all Leverkuseners over 65, informing them, among other things, of the many activities available to them.

Of course, Leverkusen also has a Home for the Aged, as well as a shortage of space inside for those who need it, and plans to eliminate this shortage. But all see as a pressing need – city, clubs and citizens – the avoidance of or delay in institutionalizing the aged. For it is precisely the senior citizen who is best off in his accustomed environment, even if this is in a new hometown.

53

Old and young

54

Sport – aces, and just for fun

Despite the many financial figures and facts, the most frequent mention of Leverkusen is found not in financial journals but on the sports pages and in sports programs. Whenever the subject is records and championships, Leverkusen is bound to figure in. There are probably more titles, medals and certificates here than in any other German city. Joke has it that the sports clubs here operate a factory. In fact, Bayer promotes the clubs from which the champions come, and the city supports proficiency sports. Few top athletes have been born in Leverkusen, by the way. They have come from everywhere else, lured by large and generous, if unaustentatious, training and competition facilities – even more, by sportstrainers who are not only extraordinarily expert in their disciplines but also aware, curious and inventive. They are also friends and mentors for the athletes. It is thus the spirit of sports that counts, interestingly enough, and not the financial support of the firm, the clubs and the community, valuable and effective as that support is. The limited but possible freedom from professional demands in order to take part in significant competitions, as well as the opportunity to be with other top athletes, is another attraction. A Leverkusen speciality was added in more recent times: the Bayer Track and Field Cooperative. It concentrates and specializes the training of athletes from six clubs (which are supported not only by the firm) and focuses efforts on best-string competition – without, however, disturbing the normal functioning of the clubs.

The interdependence of best-string and all-round sport is a fact that is likewise of general benefit to Leverkusen. Out of the general sports activities of the more than 35,000 participants, organized into nearly 100 clubs, comes a heathful striving for achievement. Practice shows that this is also true of sports for the non-organized, for sports open to everyone and for groups that meet in their taverns on the occassion of the various games. It is even true of sports for the disabled, and – obviously taking certain limitations into account – sports for children and the aged, though they have less to do with achievement than play.

In these pursuits the reputed lack of history of the young city is least valid. Shortly after the turn of the century, before sport had gained general acceptance, Bayer published a memorandum on the occasion of the founding of a gymnastics club: "There is cause to create a counterweight to office and work activity and to attempt to correct this one-sidedness through participation in gymnastics and play." The call was successful, the club was founded in 1904. It was not the first founding, although in retrospect it represents the most successful one, and it was to be even less that last. Today it is not unusual to see entire families taking part in sport after working-hours. The question whether, in Leverkusen, sport is pursued more on principle than elsewhere almost answers itself. When the Round Gymnasium, Central Competition and Training Center was opened in March 1975, there already

Leverkusen became a synonym for industry and sport. This development began shortly after the turn of the century in order to create a counterweight to work in office and factory. Today the reputation of the sport city is marked by titles and championships.
Not only highly demanding sport is the goal. There are sport activities for children as well as the handicapped. Exclusive hobbies on the one hand, sport for everyone on the other; only in this way is the picture of a "sport city" rounded out.
And in spite of all victories – the goal is never totally attained.

existed in the city more than 50 gymnasia and four indoor and five outdoor swimmingpools. According to the accompanying public announcement, the relatively late completion date underscored the city's continuing program of furtherance of sport. "Priority was and is given to active participation, to places of exercise and competition of the schools and clubs, to sport facilities in the individual suburbs."

58

A pun in German has it that it is better to celebrate fests (Feste feiern) than to work hard (feste arbeiten). The pun is often heard in Leverkusen and points to a healthful proclivity for sociability. Indeed, the inhabitants of the city, whose wages and salaries are relatively high, probably do not indulge in more merry-making than elsewhere in the Rhineland. But the fests take many forms and have a variety of origins.

The fests in the village communities in outlying areas are strongly traditional. They often point to centuries of tradition, and this includes the shooting clubs, which are found in nearly every suburb and whose historical elements continue to defy modern influence. Not quite so old but every bit as tradition-laden is Leverkusen's Carnival (i.e., Mardi Gras). At the more than a hundred fools' sessions and balls each season it becomes apparent that more than just the fools' greeting "Alaaf" has been borrowed from neighboring Cologne.
After all, the 24 Carnival societies bring forth each year not only 24 "eleven councils" (eleven-member chairmanships of the carnival societies) but also a string of pretty dance choruses, a Knight of Humor, and above all "His Madness" the Carnival Prince – they also organize, year for year, two Carnival parades. Fools on either side of the former city limits are not so crazy that they gave up one of their parades simply because of the state resolution of 1974 which brought about a merger of Leverkusen and Opladen. Consequently, the Prince of the Fifth Season here is the only Carnival Prince to parade twice through the streets of his mad realm, on Sunday through Wiesdorf and on Rose Monday (in spite of the competition from Cologne) through Opladen.

And then the clubs. What self-respecting club lets a year go by without a proper celebration? Festivals in Leverkusen are as varied as the clubs themselves. The people who poured into the city brought their local customs with them, and it is a sign of Leverkusen's openness and tolerance that they were accepted here. Foreigners living in the city are not excluded from this.
Until recently the tie to the particular suburb was typical for celebrations. Except for a few central events sponsored by Bayer AG, people tended to celebrate in Schlebusch or Bürrig, in Rheindorf or Opladen, in Hitdorf or Bergisch Neukirchen, in Steinbüchel or Wiesdorf; visitors were welcome, but the residents of each community tended to keep to themselves. The construction of the city center brought about a noticeable change. At first the Forum, which had been conceived as a cultural and social center, made for increased togetherness. Aside from the cultural offerings, dealt with elsewhere, the spatial and technical possibilities of the new structure were immensely attractive. From the Carnival societies to dance groups and schools, the clubs and societies made the leap to the larger facilities, and interested parties from the entire city area and beyond moved in. The city itself set the tone with its annual Fest in the Forum,

59

a stylish dance evening with prominent orchestras and soloists, and with its New Year's Eve Ball.

But it didn't stop there. The main shopping district, and particularly the City Hall Square, conceived with considerable fantasy and completed in 1977, became lively meeting-places for tens of thousands of people during the festival weeks. The high-point, the annual Leverkusener Week, at the beginning of October, stands under a different sign, and with considerable participation by guests from outside the city, and from foreign countries, underscores the world-openness of the city. On the other hand, the decorative water surfaces for the summery, nostalgic church fair elicited the jesting epithet "Puddle Fair." These are new and yet firmly anchored traditions, to which varying activities have been added. For these reasons – but not only these – the City Center has become a fully accepted focal point.

Whether within a large and official framework or in the family circle, Leverkuseners like to celebrate. Thus the terrace room in the Forum is the scene of many sociable and social events. At other times and on other occasions, the family garden is the best place to be.

61

Meanwhile, other celebrations have long since transcended the borders within which they had their origins – such as the Second-Hand Fair and the Retail Festival in Opladen, and particularly the "Morsbroicher Summer", initiated and organized by the city. Activities range from a band concert by the excellent brass band to pop music, which draw young and old to the Castle Park.

Thus the annual calendar of even a young city marks its high-points, in both private and public sectors. They not only bring eventful hours and days, they also contribute to a feeling of togetherness, to an integrated communal entity.

Fests and fun.

Eating and Drinking

There is no leverkusener in the sense that there are frank-furters and nürnbergers, hamburgers and königsbergers, berliners and leipzigers. So far, no one has named a sausage or meat-patty after this city. The Bergisch area and the Rhine-land, to which Leverkusen belongs, have their specialities, and they make for notable fare. But that doesn't mean that Leverkusen cuisine is simply Bergisch or Rhenish. Gastrono-mical fare ranges from delectable French dishes through an exotic Chinese and spicy Mediterranean menu to simple and rustic meals. The area offers restaurants with cultivated atmosphere and perfect service or abundant buffets as well small snackbars with or without self-service. And anyone who doesn't care to go inside can try the fare available at local fairs, which is as varied as it is tasty. This applies primarily, but not only, to the City Center and the shopping district in Opladen. In addition, it pays to try places in the suburbs and outlying districts, where culinary discoveries can also be made.

It is said that Leverkusen lies on the Cologne-equator. Within the city limits is brewed and drunk a beer typical of the Cologne area which is deliciously effervescent. It is served in slim glasses called Cologne "Stangen" and is quite different from "Alt Bier" available elsewhere; it is called simply "Kölsch". Anyone who adds the word "beer" betrays that he is a stranger to the area, which in Leverkusen signifies little. Anyone who wants to can easily make contact in the numerous inns and taverns where regular customers enjoy "hoisting one". And, of course, the best place is right at the bar. Here you can partake of the communal good-spirits or – as it occasionally happens – drown your sorrows all alone. Neighborhood pubs aren't only typical of Leverkusen, but this city of industry and workers is noted for its considerable number of them. Without them the neighborhood would be missing its focal point; cares, their spice; and the joke, its punchline.

64

…and at home? Sayings like "just the way mother used to make it" have their particular relevance in Leverkusen. The noon or evening meal most readily betrays the origin of the family, or at least of grandma and grandad. Whether Silesian paradise, Bohemian beer cutlet, Bavarian scones, Thuringian dumplings or Rhenish sauerbraten – recipes for local or favorite specialities were brought with the people who migrated here – or they come from a neighbor with whom recipes have been traded. Grocers and spice-dealers know well the variety of ingredients required by their patrons, particularly when families try to reproduce the good meal they had during their last holiday or vacation. But for this purpose there are the foreign specialty shops, whose customers include more than just foreigners. People learn from, and respect, each other.

Eating and drinking.

Fun at the maypole:
Sociable Society, Hitdorf.

Group(ed)

Who can count the clubs and groups, can name all the activities that have been fostered in Leverkusen since Leverkus and particularly Bayer came to the Rhine? Anyone who doesn't find an amenable group here doesn't want one, or he's looking for company without a group–and he'll find it too.

Games and songs at the Morsbroicher Summer in the Castle Park. Every year many musical groups entertain large crowds.

For the numismatists, the coin collectors, money becomes an object of exchange.

A traditon is preserved with Colts and rifles: Silver Lake Pioneers.

Competition at the Poodle Club.
Who is the fairest in the land?

The Diving Club in (demonstration)
action.

The main thing is to fly, with or
without motor: the Bayer Air Sport
Club has its own airport.

Foreigners who live in the city
belong too, of course: Greeks
grilling.

In many parts of the city, marksmen's clubs preserve old customs.

No one quite knows why Leverkusen has become a fishing center.

The railway enthusiasts "Flügelrad" in Opladen constitute a pleasant off-shoot of the tradition-rich Federal Railway Maintenance Plant.

Small, but seaworthy and exact copies of the originals: the boats of the Model Construction Club "Neptun".

The traditional dance group
"d'Trauntaler" brings Upper Bavaria
to the Rhine.

Not only loud but successful as
well – the Motor Sport Club.

Bidding high: the Skat Club.

Wet and colorful fun; for a change,
in front of the City Hall:
Rhine Wupper Windsurfing Club.

Group(ed)

Green for the eye, lungs and stomach

Anyone driving through Leverkusen when the flora is in bloom will hardly suspect he is in a metropolis or industrial city. The city boundary runs in fact through the Bergische Obstkammer (fruit storeroom), and the harvests of apples, pears, plums and even strawberries provide a substantial adjunct to the farmer's income. Nevertheless, local agriculture – about a third of the area of Leverkusen is under the plow – is preponderently field agriculture. To this are added 42 hectars of garden cultivation and above all the some ten per cent of the land – unusual for a metropolitan area – covered by forest.

It is little wonder that 40 per cent of agricultural undertakings keep dairy cows, every other one raises beef and every third, poultry. After all, the customers are close by, and so most of the beef, pork, poultry and eggs, fruit and vegetables remains right in the city. Travellers see the "For Sale" signs near the farms offering their produce, and may notice that most of the farms stand alone amid meadows and fields. All this is to the advantage of the housewife in her weekly shopping.

In an area where industry and trade require so many personnel, agricultural wages are substantially high. For this reason, small and middle-size family farms are typical. Statistically speaking, on each of the 88 farms, of which, by the way, only seven are operated as a sideline, there is just an average of two personnel. This is a surprising figure to the layman, considering that area of the 2,600 hectars of green and fields is eight times as great as the Bayer Works, with its 37,000 employees. Were it not for their high efficiency and the necessary machinery, the farms could not make a go of it.

The situation is similar for the 32 truck garden enterprises in Leverkusen, in which, besides the 40 proprietors and family members, a mere hundred additional workers are employed. Twenty-seven horticultural enterprises have specialized in flowers and tree nursuries. They raise almost two-thirds of the flowers sold in Leverkusen; few metropolises are so self-sufficient. This picture is different for cultivation of vegetables. While some plants are cultivated in the city, cauliflower, red cabbage, peas and carrots, beans and other vegetables are "imported".

The enormous growth of the population has led to a reduction, since 1950, of the area used for agriculture and gardens. Still, the Rhineland Agricultural Chamber found that there was no major damage to the landscape. It reported, in fact: "The structure and number of agricultural and garden enterprises that continue to exist offer the best guarantee that the landscape of Leverkusen will maintain in the future the variety and beauty they now enjoy."

Even though house gardens have been plentiful in both old and new Levekusen from the beginning, there just aren't enough gardens to go round. There are more than a thousand garden-plots in eleven areas, but twice that many would not suffice. Particularly the people who streamed in from far corners of the earth wanted to have their own plot of ground. The largest garden area, in Ruhlach in Opladen, comprises 188 plots; the smallest, in the settlement Mathildenhof, 26.
The city is planning 16 additional garden areas. The intent is not only to satisfy would-be gardners but to add, in an easy and practical way, to the total greenery of the city.

74

The boys and girls of the suburb Rheindorf never tire of it: looking into the mirror and giggling at their distorted reflection. Who thinks of art or of Vojin Bakics? His "Fun Sculpture" belongs as much to the Eulengasse School as, a little farther on, Bernhard Luginbühl's Steel Giraffe belongs to the Netzestrasse School or Marino di Teana's seemingly functional "Plastic Building" to the Professional School. So too, a person walking past Henri Nouveau's monument in the park of the City Hospital need not think of a "Bach Fuge" (photo below left). Human encounter with contemporary sculpture seems intentionless but is based nevertheless on a cleverly contrived concept. Art in conjunction with construction was seen as a special tasks in the stormy developmental years of Leverkusen. It was part of every public building and was planned along with it. There thus came into being, aside from free-standing sculptures, the great window of Georg Meistermann in the Lise Meitner Gymnasium and the transparent wall of Francois Chapuis in the Freiherr vom Stein Gymnasium.

The most convincing example of combined art with architecture: the Agam Hall, in the Forum, named after the Israeli Yaacov Agam. He conceived the triangular folded aluminum panels of the six walls, in 387 shades of color, achieving exemplary work of kinetic art (photos next page over). And therein, concert and show, lecture and discussion, conference and dance.

A few minutes' walk distant, on the City Hall Square, is the Acquamobile, by Gottfried Gruner, in its own way an integral part of the architecture. The 10-meter-high steel sculpture moves not only water but also the phantasy of the viewer, distracting him from the hectic surroundings. Art in everyday life – it's found throughout the city, and a tour of it would require a complicated map.; but what average visitor would find such a map useful?

Thus the idea of somehow bringing all these "secretly" hoarded artworks together (such as Norbet Kricke's towering Steel Dissonance in front of the Doktorsburg) is not too removed. Any such plan would, of course, compete with the original conception, according to which art and architecture should mingle with one another. And yet, such a plan does exist. The park surrounding Morsbroich Castle–following this

idea–could become an open-air museum, a sculpture or art park amid stands of old trees. A charming idea, particularly since it is unique for the Federal Republic.

Through discussions concerning modern art, Morsbroich has set standards for cultural development in Leverkusen. It found, and finds, recognition in the art world not only for its significant changing exhibits but also for its notable art possessions.

Such a sculpture-park is part of a comprehensive plan for the renovation and partial restructuring of Morsbroich Castle and adjacent structures arranged in a half-circle. In 1951 the Castle was made over into a city museum. According to the museum charter, it was to give "the cultural life of the city an opportunity to extend into new areas".

The hexagonal Agam Hall in the Forum is an art center itself–for concerts, discussions, theater, dance fetes…The Israeli artist Yaacov Agam conceived the triangular folded aluminum panels of the six walls, in 387 shades of color, achieving an exemplary work of kinetic art.

Art in everyday life.

Between Green and Gray: the City Center

The City Park and the Dhünn meadow were there before the city was, as was the industry on the other side. That the city lies between has hardly any historical relevance. The location is rather (where else is there something comparable?) the result of a sober examination, of a report drawn up by city and traffic planners brought in from the outside. The area next to the Wiesdorf town hall they found to be "the most suitable – large enough and having almost no construction". Almost. For, after all, the mentioned town hall was here, housing the Council and the Administration; also here was the main street, which had developed one-sidedly into a chain of display windows. That was nevertheless a starting point. There were also expanses of green, with apartment houses in the English garden-city style, as one still finds it about the City Center today. By the way, the English word "city": Elsewhere in Germany this word means the old quarter. In Wiesdorf the old quarter was pushed to one side by the construction of the City Center – and became a problem-child. The new downtown was to be, from the outset, more than the main shopping district, more than the concentration of administration and services, more than the goal of those hungry for art and culture. It was to be all of these; it was to be a place of encounter for the entire population. Goals apparently have to be set so high in order to reach the possible – and the efforts were not in vain.

78

Anyone who strolls through the six department stores, then past the display windows of the old shops, and ambles by 60 new shops – anyone who takes a seat in one of the many restaurants – no longer sees utopia. He also has no idea of what courage to take risks, without guiding example, was involved in city planning and enterprise for a project of this magnitude. The successful attempt to transform daring thought into deed makes clear that out of what had been a factory with a small town there emerged a self-confident city. The throw of the lasso represented by Cologne's new plan for incorporation brought nothing. Of course, as improvisation came to an end, so did the are of superlatives. The achievement could not be repeated.

Not only the necessities of life but the profane, the commercial find room in the City Center. The versatile "landscape" of City Hall Square is also the scene of merry-making.

A little too low but broad and portly, the City Hall stands out in the landscape of residential and commercial buildings, of towers and pylons. It is not an edifice of magnificence, like those once created by proud, confident burghers as an expression of their striving for power and culture. Rather it is a center for services, dedicated to functionalism. An ingenious information system helps citizens find their way in this administrative construction, of necessity neutral and sober, with three of its five floors consistently designed as a huge office, as an "office landscape." This conception repels some, but with proper furnishings, lighting and acoustics it has its advantages. In any case, the City Hall, with its space for some 650 employees, evidences interesting examples of modern office design.

Leverkusen-Central – railway station for long-distance and commuter trains, for train and bus traffic in happy proximity. Schedules list about 80 departures for trains and over 700 for the 27 bus lines. And still, strangers have to be able to find their way around this complex. A system of orientation employing large-format and smaller direction-finders makes it possible – signs that become more detailed as a traveler nears his departure point. The inviting information pavillion dispenses additional information. The junction for public transportation, including taxis, is maintained in a friendly green and is a calling card of the city. From here it is not far to the shopping district and to the City Hall, to public performances and events, to congresses in the Forum, and, finally, to the Stadium and other sports facilities.

81

Between green and gray: the City Center.

City Center Fest

The new possibilities of the new City Center were a challenge to the development of new traditions. One of the new events is an annual "Puddle Fest", patterned on old-style fairs, and named, in modest humor, after the decorative water surfaces of City Hall Square. "Leverkusen Weeks" already existed before the city center was completed. But it was not until the creation of the versatile open area in the center that it took on its special flavor. Merry-making goes on for days, people mingle in the big tent, in the Forum, and above all outside where visiting groups perform–each year from a different region, usually from another country. There have been musicians, folk-music groups, and performers with specialities from the neighboring Bergisch Land, from Berlin and Bavaria. Home-grown ensembles have taken part, along with the most varied troupes formed by the foreign groups who live in the city. Finally, guests from Finland, Great Britain, Denmark, Yugoslavia, Austria and–as the photos show–from the Netherlands have given the Leverkusen Weeks their particular accent.

82

The flea market is always popular. Year after year, during Leverkusen Weeks, hundreds of people turn in goods that have been lying around the house, and thousands of prospective customers come to gawk and shop.

Some forty girls dance with verve and precision to the music of their own band: Koninklijk Show Drum en Majorettenkorps "The Arno's".

Kids turn out in droves for the children's fests, and enthusiastically make music, sing, build and paint. Things wouldn't be complete without a contest in genuine Dutch wooden shoes.

Children's Circus "Akivo"–
Children display finesse and phantasy, for adults too.

The instruments are Scottish, the musicians are Dutch, the name of their group, Idaho Company, is English, and they're performing for a German audience.
Leverkusen international.

Old pros performing Black country blues at a jam session at dusk–another regular feature of the traditional City Volksfest in autumn.

Always popular: folklore, homegrown and from other countries. Here, a school group from Maastricht.

The Forum, created in an expand-
able triangular pattern, combines
many functions in its architecture by
Ulrich S. von Altenstadt. The range
from theater performances and
concerts, balls and congresses,
to exhibitions and educational
activities.

The stage of the Great Hall can be
adapted to the varying needs of
visiting theater groups.
Leverkusen has no ensemble of its
own.

Variety in the Forum – plan and reality

Forum – the name was a program which had as its model the imperial fora of ancient Rome, whose squares and markets were surrounded by constructions with many different functions. The plan was to have a grouping of public facilities arranged about an inviting open-space: auditoriums of various sizes for many purposes, theater and adult education, youth center and city library, museum and music school. It can be seen in its entirety in the form of a model. Only the first phase of construction has been realized – the square and the Grand Auditorium bordering it, a completely workable unity. Its situation is that of a traffic island, surrounded by autobahn, city street and railway, and thus readily accessible. It is only a few minutes' walk from the bus and train stations. Cars can drive directly under the building into two parking tiers. At the opening, on 20 September 1969, the then Minister President of North-Rhine Westphalia, Heinz Kühn, stated: "The Leverkusen Forum can be a major cultural filling station between the depots Cologne and Düsseldorf". He wasn't thinking of the traffic situation, and certainly not the final Forum planning. Kühn was alluding rather to the concept of the house, whose perfect stage facilities do not serve a Leverkusen theater ensemble. As a theater for guest performances it quickly set standards that inspired the slogan, "in the Forum there's always a festival". In the meantime, a cultural program comprising first-class concert and ballet performances, good theater and opera evenings, established a niveau that is fully acceptable even to an increasingly critical public. Keen audience interest together with abstention from a costly local theater ensemble permits a high level of quality, though the city subsidy is below the average of that paid by cities of comparable size.

In addition to superior theater, opera and concerts in the Grand Auditorium and other rooms, the public is served by conferences and congresses, balls and entertainment in the Terrace Room, exhibits in the foyers, and an objective program of adult education. Millions of visitors, many from the suburbs as well, have "tanked up" here on knowledge, sociability, and good spirits.

But the Forum did not bring the first guest performances to Leverkusen. Bayer, with its own theatrical performances and concerts, has a long tradition of cultivation of the arts. Performances in the firm's own Recreation House, and those in the Forum, constitute a challenge to the city. Both organizers pretty much have their own publics, but they supplement each other. All in all, the cultural life of the city is of significance equal to that of larger cities, and in many cases even greater.

Cultural offerings in the Forum range from theater for children, such as that of the Leverkusen ensemble Ömmes and Oimel,

to outstanding ballet, opera, operette and theater performances by German and foreign companies,

whose Leverkusen guest performances are often regular features of the season. There are thus ties to the hosting theater and its public.

86

Artistry-in-miniature of international repute, of which the French mime Marcel Marceau is an exponent,

is as much a part of the Forum program as a song-evening by the politico-bard Wolf Biermann, or a satirical cabaret.

Not least of the bright spots are concerts by orchestras of international renown; above, a concert with composer Hans-Werner Henze on the podium.

Public with a distinct character:
It is appreciative and capable of
enthusiasm, particularly since, for
many, the Forum fully opened to
them the world of stage and podium.
Beyond that it is critical and
objective; for the changing guest
performances confront it with ample
opportunity for comparison.
The novel finds the same skeptical
curiosity here as it does elsewhere.

Rich variety in the Forum

visited. People of all ages and of the most varied interests and motivations visit this tiny world of enchantment. It harbors a richness of exotic and native flora. Botanists can discover here dwarf-conifers, bamboo grasses, papyrus shrubs, irises, calla, witch hazel, ornamental cherry and many other rare plants. The entire Japanese Garden is surrounded by water. Red, yellow and withe water-lillies gently rock on the water-surface. Access is to be had only via one of the bridges and through the toriis (Japanese gate), which is guarded by fierce, bronze temple-dogs.

This jewel was laid out by the builder of the Bayer Concern in Leverkusen, Privy Councillor Carl Duisberg. In 1912 he engaged Japanese garden architects who laid out the first Japanese garden where today the 31-story high-rise stands. The dwarf had to give in to the giant when, in 1960, the building was constructed: The garden was removed 200 meters to its present location.

Bridges over Water, Rails, Streets

There are exactly 202 bridges in Leverkusen. That's a good half of the number in Venice. But, unlike the city of lagoons, not even half of them lead over water. On the other hand the two cities, so unlike otherwise, have one thing in common: They would be unthinkable without bridges. The Wupper and the Dhünn flow through Leverkusen, to say nothing of many brooks. Three autobahns, two of which are among the most traveled in Germany, cut across the city area. The tracks of four stretches of railroad run straight through the city. What would Leverkusen be without its bridges?
Under these spans there are a few picturesque old structures, here and there, still, the brick tunnels dating from the earliest date of the railroads, models of which one frequently finds in play-rooms. But the bridges that serve transport have a limited life. For that reason – and also for the reason that so many new over- and underpasses became necessary – the style of our times dominates, with sometimes imposingly intricate concrete ribbons lightly suspended, or structures boring in their functional orientation. Of much more signi-ficance than questions of style, however, are the circumstan-ces that emerge from such a frequency of bridges. It is hard to make a coherent city-structure from an area so cut up, and it is quite amazing the way a virtue was made of necessity. The "islands" resulting from the criss-crossing of streams and traffic arteries became settlements of quite convenient proportions, bordered by green areas, on the one hand, and on the other, by a generous, well planned network of roads connecting the settlements with each other, with the down-town area and with places of work. Unfortunately, the entire project is by no means complete; the city, in many places, is caught in a conflict between cultivation of green areas and plans for construction.

90

Elegantly conceived bridges help traffic surmount natural obstacles, such as that over the pond near Mathildenhof, and – of substantially different proportions – the autobahn bridge over the Rhine.

Greater contrast than that offered by the photos on this page is difficult to imagine, although both bridges serve, or should serve, pedestrians. Left, a modern steel construction for crossing railway tracks in Opladen. Below, a remnant of yesterday at Morsbroich Castle.

Traffic on three levels: Pedestrians, through traffic and cross traffic pass smoothly without disturbing each other.

Like spaghetti on a fork, cloverleaf accesses between two of the three autobahns that meet in Leverkusen.

With the romance of a toy train, a railway overpass in Bergisch Neukirchen.

Technical progress and thoughtful nature meet here.

Modern constructions: Connection between two buildings of Bayer AG, over Federal highway 8 (left), and Y-bridge for pedestrians over the two-tier city autobahn in the City Center.

Bridges

There are many more stories that could be told and pictures that could be shown of the singular city of Leverkusen. For it is characteristic of the city that it is not a frozen historical monument with heroes and dates to be learned by heart, but, instead, a continually changing structure and a many-sided living area in which different types of people and opinions have their place. Room enough for its own stories and pictures. This collection is, and must remain, incomplete.